MERRY MONOLOGUES

A LAUGH FOR EVERY
DAY IN THE YEAR

BY
MARY MONCURE PARKER

CHICAGO
T. S. DENISON & COMPANY
PUBLISHERS

Merry Monologues

PREFACE

REALIZING the difficulty experienced by the Public Reader in obtaining suitable material, the author of Merry Monologues has yielded to repeated requests and presents in this little volume, for the first time in printed form, a selected list of her most successful Readings. These selections are wholly original, and bear the stamp of enthusiastic public approval. They have been rendered successfully throughout this country and England and she has appeared under the auspices of Mr. Gustave Frohman.

Taken from a wide repertoire, they are sufficiently varied in character and sentiment to enable the Reader to make up a well-rounded program in which high comedy mingles with farce and pathos in a manner suitable for all occasions. In addition are included a number of new Monologues, written especially for this volume—which never have been given in public. There are also included several

5

poems, a few of which have already appeared in print and are here given through the courtesy of *The Chicago Herald*.

These verses are especially adapted to that particular form of entertainment, called the pianologue, viz., reading to music.

The author sends forth this group of readings and monologues in full confidence that the Reader who uses them will receive the same enthusiastic response, the same spontaneous expression of approval that has always greeted her in her years before the public as a Professional Reader.

NOTE.—Many Readers play only chords for musical readings. The author merely suggests the various airs because she has used them successfully; perhaps other music, more suitable, may be found. Do not attempt in every instance to fit the words of the music to the words of the poem, but play the air as a running accompaniment, fast or slow as desired.

CONTENTS

ON THE STREET CAR

ʊ ʊ̆ ʊ

CHARACTERS:

MASIE, *an exclusive passenger.*

MAUDE, *a friend.*

THE OTHER PASSENGERS, *a horrid crowd.*

SCENE—*On a street car at the rush hour, going home.*

MASIE, *emphatically:*

Come on, Maud, you'll have to push to get on this car. My, what a crowd! Did you ever see such a lot of boors? How they push. I'll pay. I have the change right here! No, no, you musn't pay. I'll get it in a minute. What's that, conductor? Other people waiting? Well, goodness sake, everybody has to wait! Oh, didn't you pay, Maud? I thought you got ahead of me while I was talking to that conductor, I'll get the change.

Dear me, this clasp sticks so! Oh, Maud, don't pay! There! Here it is. A five-dollar bill! I thought I had change. What's that, conductor? Can't change it? I never heard of such a thing. The idea! Oh, Maud, you'll pay? Well, I'll pay you back. No seats, of course. Heavens! How these people push!

That matinee was so late—and then the tea after. But we had a lovely time. Lovely music, wasn't it? Please don't prod my back, madam. Well, you don't have to lean on me. Gracious, my feet are so tired.

The men in this car certainly are polite —not. That grouch standing next to you, Maud, is mad because your feathers stick in his face. Mercy, how these people crowd! Why don't they wait for the next car? Serves us right for not taking a taxi. Isn't this villianous service on this road? I'll have papa write a letter of complaint to the company tomorrow.

Did you hear that fresh man, Maud? He said he bet the company would be scared of papa. Too bad to have to mix with such persons.

Wasn't the leading man adorable, Maud? Oh, my feet are so tired! This is a positive crush, I can't stand another minute. Oh, Maud, quick, that man got up to give us a seat. No, you take it. No, I positively won't—you take it, I insist. Why, madam, that man gave me that seat. The very idea of your taking it.

10

Get up right away. Not so as I could notice it? Some people have positively no manners. Serves us right for riding with the masses. Isn't this stuffy, Maud? I shall faint. Madam, you must not prod me in the back.

Oh, Maud, look at the sign! We've taken the wrong car. Gracious, wasn't that a stupid conductor not to know what car we wanted? We must get right off, Maud. For goodness sake move, you people, so we can get by.

Conductor, we want transfers. What! Only issue them when we pay fare? This is an outrage. I'll report you tomorrow. Thank heaven we are going to get off this car! Did you hear that brute, Maud? He said everybody else would thank heaven, too. Conductor, why don't you stop this car? We did not tell you to? You ought to have known we wanted to get off. Next time we won't take your old car—We'll go by the "L." So, there!

THE RENAISSANCE OF THE KISS

("Home, Sweet Home" is the air suggested when this poem is given as a pianologue.)

Why don't you kiss her in the morning
    when you say good-by?
It may be somewhat difficult, but then
    suppose you try.
Perhaps she wears an old kimono, and her
    hair in kids,
And she looks so unattractive that Cupid's
    auto skids.
But, old fellow, just remember that you
    are no Apollo,
Although that statement may be rather
    hard for you to swallow.
You've grown quite bald, and very red,
    and goodness!—paunchy, too.
Though she is weather-beaten, Old Time
    has whacked at you.
Don't you recall that when you married
    she was "a stunning gal"?
Her temper's sharp, but, after all, she's
    been a dandy pal.
From grinding bread and butter cares,
    romance is apt to fly.
Well, then—just kiss her in the morning
    when you say good-by.

HUSBANDS IS HUSBANDS

℧ ℧ ℧

CHARACTERS:

MANDY JACKSON, *who has loved and supported four.*

LIZA JOHNSING, *a helper and a quiet listener.*

SCENE—*In close proximity to the wash-tub.*

MANDY JACKSON *elucidates:*

Hit suttingly was a foolish pusson what said dat matches is made in heaven, Liza Johnsing. Mos' likely dey is 'ranged whar dey makes de sulpher kind, an' you kin' guess whar dat is. I ain't sayin'. I done had four husbands, an' wa'n't none of 'em wuth shakin' a stick at, much less takin' up St. Peter's time rangin' weddin's fer 'em.

De fust time I was married jest fifteen minutes. De man's name was Alexander. Dat was a fine name, but de man—um—umph—, honey! Ef you had de powder an' shot an' de gun all loaded, dat man wa'n't wuth even de effort hit would take to lif' de gun an' shoot him. He somehow got a notion I had money, an' soon as

15

we got married, dat man axed me to loan him two dollars.

I says, "Look heah man, I 'spect you to take keer of me, I ain't gwine to suppote you, you shif'less bag of bones."

Well, he said, " 'Scuse me a minute, I want to speak to a man outside." Fur all I know, Liza, he's lookin' fur dat man yit, fur he never come back. I was a young nigger den, an' I hadn't learnt dat de reason a man gits married is kase he 'spects to git supported. Dat knowledge comes with 'sperience. De second one I collected was a pretender. He could make out he was doin' mo' work an' do less than any man I ever see. He could spend all mawnin' beatin' a little two by fo' rug. He'd beat a little while, an' den he'd res' an' den he'd beat a little while longer, an' den rest up agin.

"Cleanliness is nex' to Godliness," he used to say. I ain't tole you he used to be a preacher, fo' I married him. He suttinly had a fine eddication. Why, Liza, he could take all the compartments of a word an' 'splanify the meanin'. He had a fine eddication but not much execution. Yes, dat's what he would say when I'd

16

jaw him 'bout de time he'd take imitatin' work.

"De Bible say, Mandy, dat 'Cleanliness is nex' to Godliness.' Clean, dat means keepin' ev'thing washed up an' tidy. Li—dat means you musn't lie bout hit—an' Ness, dat's a Latin word dat compromises hit all an' means dat you jes' got to do ev'thing thorough an' not shirk or you goin' to git into trouble. Dat's de reason dat I takes my time 'bout doin' things, I'se thorough."

He suttinly knowed a lot and he could argify by the hour. Dat nigger was sho' eddicated, but he hated wuk. Jes' as I say he had a fine eddication but not no execution. We never had but one fuss Liza but dat suttin was some combustion. He got to arguin' one day kase I axed him to hep me hang some clothes on the line an' he argufied an' argufied while I was doin' the wuk. Finally I got mad an' I let out on him an' I wuked my jaw fur ten minutes straight.

"Woman, woman," he says when he could git a word in edgeways, "You don' reason. No woman kin reason. She kin jes' wuk her mouf 'thout thinkin' what's comin' out. What's needed in ev'ry house-

hold is a arbittrator. Yes a arbittrator.
Dat's a Latin word meanin'—"

"Don' want to heah none of yo' Dago
words," I busts out, pickin' up the stick
I uses when I boils the clothes, "De nex'
argymint we gits into 'twon't be no arbittrator we'll need, hit'll be the undertaker,
an' I'll be the one that'll call him in, an'
don' you fergit it."

I mus' have made an impression on dat
nigger, kase he quit argufyin' an' one day
when I come home from wuk, he had lit
out, an' I never seen hide nor hair of him
no mo'. Dat remines me of something
queer, Liza. Hit happened when I was
wukin' at de Martin's. You know dem
fokes what lives at dat pretty little bung-
aloo on de lake front. A cullud gemmen
come along an' axed Mis' Martin ef he
could empty ashes. She was one of dem
ladies dat allus hangs roun' de laundry
when you is washin' fer fear you is gwine
to loaf an' she won't git her money's wuth.
She says, "Mandy, what you keep starin'
at dat man fer so hard, when he goes
back an' fo'th wid de ashes, like you never
seen nobody befo'?"

"Lawsy, Mis' Martin," I says, "Dat

18

man suttinly looks familiar to me. I sho'
believe he was mah first husband."

I suttin sho' believe dat nigger heard
me, tho' he never let on, kase when he
went out with his nex' bucket of ashes,
he never come back; not even to git his
money. Now we gits to the third speci-
men in mah collection, Liza. He was a
sickly pusson, mo' like a baby dan a full
growed man, but he was good-natured an'
puttered roun' de house keepin it kin' of
tidy when I was away an' den he was
harmless. He only lived a few yeahs
after we was married and I says to mahsef
when he died, "I'm gwine to give dat man
a fine funeral." You see Liza hit was de
fust time I had a chanst to bury a husband
an' I wanted to do hit right.

Ole Mose, dat's mah present man, he jes'
lost his wife de day befo', an we planned
to have a gran' double funeral. We had
dem two castors settin' side by side, fine
velvet castors wid silver handles on 'em.
Dem two suttin looked kin' of peaceful
an' pitiful layin' dere, wid flowers all
roun' 'em. They never seen each other
when they was livin', kase Mose only
moved to our neighborhood 'bout two
weeks 'fore she died. She done had one

19

of them political strokes, the day after she moved an' she never moved after.

Ev'body we knowed come to that bury-in'. Dar was six carriages an' one man come in a automobeel. Dat suttinly was some funeral. We put two bunches of crepe on de do', an' dah was sho' some moanin' an' groanin'. Ev'body seemed to want to do nuff wailin' fer bofe to wunst. Hit suttin was a gran' funeral.

Well, Liza, dat was how I come to marry Mose. He used to come ovah an' talk 'bout his departed wife, kase he was so lonesome an' one evenin' he say:

"Mandy, me an' you is forsaken pus-sons, all 'lone in this heah cole ole worl' (he suttinly could 'spress hisself awful nice, Mose could). 'Sposen we enters de marriage 'lationships."

An' I says, wid a sort of careless 'spres-sion, like I wa'n't too anxious, "Oh, I don' min' if we does."

You see, Liza, I hadn't had nobody to purvide fer, fer some time an' I was kin' of gittin' my han' out. We was married very simple 'thout no fuss an' feathers. After you bin a bride three times, ain't nothin' very pealin' 'bout a weddin' veil. Mose jes' walked over to whar mah married 'sticate was hangin' an' rubs out mah las' husband's name an' writes in his'n, Mose Walker.

Our preacher was callin' dat evenen' an' he say, "You can't do dat kase dat ain't no regulation mar'iage."

So I had to haul out de old weddin' veil again an' we stood up an' he mar'ied us de nex' day when Mose got a new license an' I made a cake.

Mose is a good ole soul an' we don't have many quar'els. Course he don' wuk but den you can't 'spec a man to wuk. He's been mighty thoughtful 'bout gittin' me several places to do washin' an' clean-in' an' we gits along very harmonicum.

I believe in de Bible, Liza Johnsing, an' I'se a great chu'ch-goer, but dat's one thing I can't quite swaller an' dat's whar de Good Book says dat man shall earn his bread by the sweat of his brow. Dat sut-tinly is some mistake. All de men I has had, has earnt de bread by de puspiration of mah brow. Dey suttinly ain't done much sweatin' count of wuk. An' dat's de Gawd's trufe I'm tellin' you Liza Johnsing, sho's you bawn.

OH, FRIEND OF MINE

*("In the Gloaming" or "Massenet's Elegy" are the airs
suggested when this poem is given as a pianologue.)*

I clasp your little hand, oh, friend of
    mine!
We talk of matters of the day,
Of happenings along the way,
And that is all we say,
        Oh, friend of mine!

I look into your eyes, oh, friend of mine!
Then to my gaze there comes to view
That mystic, wondrous, inner you,
Shining through orbs of blue,
        Oh. friend of mine!

Tho' held apart by fate, oh, friend of
    mine!
That blessed look is all my own,
That look unto the world unknown,
Thank God, is mine alone,
        Oh, friend of mine!

GEORGE'S FIRST SWEET-HEART

ზ   ზ   ზ

CHARACTERS:

GEORGE, *who experiences a change of heart.*

THE BLUE EYED GIRL, *of the dancing school.*

SCENE—*Christmas Day at the home of the Blue Eyed Girl.*

GEORGE *confides:*

Say, if there's anything I allus hated it's dancin' school. It's all right fer girls, but I'd rather play ball or skate. 'Tain't so bad this winter 'cause there's a little girl that goes to our club—well, I never liked girls much, but this one, she's diff'runt. She ain't like nobody I ever seen, with blue eyes an' long curls an' when I say, "Aw, I can't dance that," she says she'll show me, just as perlite. Why I don't like girls is 'cause my sisters is girls. They're all older 'n me an' they're always coppin' Pa's and Ma's job an' telling me how to behave an' what's my dooty or snitchin' on me to the folks.

23

But, anyhow, this little girl—well, the way I first saw her was, I was out walkin' with my dog Buzz an' Buzz he busted away from me an' commenced to fight with her dog, an' she screamed an' I called Buzz off. She tooked her dog in her arms an' says jest as sweet, in the kind of tone Ma has when I'm sick or when she comes an' looks at me when I'm 'sleep an' she don't think I'm listenin'. Well, she says to her dog with a tremblin' voice, "Oh you poor Tiny." An' I says, "Aw, Buzz never hurt your dog," kind of rough, but I was sorry, an' I didn't want no girl to know it. Then she looked up to me an' gee, she had the bluest eyes I ever seen. The kids calls eyes, lamps, but hers was just eyes, an' that was the first time I seen her, and I ain't felt the same since.

Well Christmas, I tooked her a box of candy. When I got to her door I was most ready to run away but I stuck to the ship, like Com'dore Perry what's in our hist'ry or the boy on the burnin' deck, only the steps wasn't burnin' an' if they was, the snow would of put out the fire, but they wasn't.

I went in the house when the hired girl, she come to the door. Then my gir—I mean the girl I was tellin' you about, she come down, I seen her peekin' over the stairs first. Oh, I ain't told you what her handle was, I mean her name, it's Lurabelle. Some name, bullieve me!

Well, she come down an' I was standin' in the parlor where the hired girl put me. An' she says, "Merry Christmus, George," an' I says, "Merry Christmus," but I didn't say her name, cause it's too long, anyhow. I never said no more but just stuck the candy box at her, 'cause my throat got all dry an' I near choked so I didn't say nothin,' an' she says, "Oh, George, that's jest grand. Sit down," an' I set down on the edge of a chair an' I wriggled my cap in my hand. Then she set down on another chair an' kinder smoothed out her dress an' she says, "It's Christmus, ain't it?" an' I says, "Yes, it's Christmus." An' she says, "I like Christmus, don't you?" an' I says, "Yes, it's bull—I mean, I like it all right." I most said "bully," but I didn't get it out. An' she says, "I got a doll an' a doll piano an' a hat an' a muff an' some pitscher books an' this candy—" An' I says, "Aw, the candy ain't nothin'.' But it was somethin' 'cause it costed all my money, that

I put in my bank an' was savin' for skates. They said Santa Claus was goin' to bring me some skates. Just as though you didn't know the guff about Santa Claus an' that it's really your Pa an' Ma 'at gives you presents, but it pleases them to think you bullieve it an' so I don't keer if it pleases 'em.

Well, about the girl, we was talkin' an' gettin' along fine when I looked up an' seen her whole fambly peekin' through the hangin's from the next room, like we was a show, we two an' I says in a hurry, "I must go" an' I got so fussed that I slipped on the rug an' darn near fell down. Fambly's is all mutts. They think they runs everything. Still, I guess I'll go to dancin' school all winter.

You know I don't pay much 'tention to her, that girl I mean, outside of dancin' school cause the fellers is such rubes, they'd holler, "Oh, George is gotter girl, George is gotter girl," an' bullieve me if they did, I'd smash their slats in. So I pertend at day school I'm a woman-hater. I used to be onct really, but I ain't no more. I heard Ma say to Pa the other night, "George is gettin' more civerlized. He likes dancin' school this year." That's a queer way to talk about me 'cause our gogafy says, white races is civerlized an' black races is saverges an' I bullong to the white race all right. Ma gits mixed sometimes, I think, 'cause she ain't went to school fer so long. Say, her eyes is jist as blue, my girl—the girl's I mean, I was tellin' you about—Gee, whiz!

BOBBY AND THE NEW BABY

("Rock-a-bye, Baby," is the air suggested when this poem is given as a pianologue.)

They told me that my nose is broked,
    I'm feelin' it all day
Seems des like it always did,
    I don't care what they say.

Guess maybe they are foolin' me.
    Well, does you know, up stairs
There's the funny wrinkled baby
    What I asked for in my prayers?

A little baby sister!
    But they made a big mistake,
An' when I asked my daddy
    If he would please to take

Her back an' get a new one
    That was pretty, smooth an' white,
He only laughed an' kissed me,
    But I pray real hard each night,

For a better lookin' baby,
    I'm des so shamed of this,
That I shake my head when nursie
    Says, "Give sister a sweet kiss."

They say, "Oh, Bobby's jealous
    An' his nose is broked in two,
But I ain't. I'm disserpointed
    'Cause our baby isn't new.

29

LUCILE GETS READY FOR A DANCE

ზ ზ ზ

CHARACTERS:

LUCILE, *who does the talking.*

HER PATIENT MOTHER AND SISTER, *who help her.*

TOMMY, *the small brother, who hinders her.*

MR. SAUNDERS, *who bears her away in triumph.*

SCENE—*Home of most any debutante.*

LUCILE *sputters:*

Oh, dear, there's a button off my white gloves, the only long pair that's clean. Mother, please sew it on,—Bess, won't you fix my hair? It looks like fury. Yes, I've taken it down again. I wouldn't wear it that way to a dog fight. Oh, Mother, don't fuss about my slang now. I'm all nerves. I know it's a quarter to eight. Don't tell me again, please, Bess. Gracious, you're pulling my hair—well, don't preach, Bess. You ought to write sermons on always doing just right. Of course if I'd been all ready and so forth

31

and so forth, I know it all by heart.
There, my hair looks better, but it isn't
right yet. Oh, thanks. Criminy, Jacobs!
Where is my opera bag? Mother, please
find it and put my slippers in it.

Bess, lift this gown over my head so I
won't muss my hair. Oh, yes, please, of
course please, that's understood, and will
you hook it up—*please*. Don't say it's
late again, *please*. Didn't we have a
sorority meeting this afternoon and I
couldn't get away? Tommy, let my vanity
case alone and go right out of this room.
Mother, make Tommy go out. You're a
naughty boy. Oh, Mother, do make him
go out or I'll go distracted. Oh, Mother,
not those slippers—my white ones. You
can't find them? I'll bet Amy took them
to the house party. I wish she'd let my
things alone. They'll be all soiled when
she comes back. Where's my opera cloak?
Oh, look how soiled that is—positively
black. Bess, let me wear your new one.
You aren't going. Well, you might let
me wear it, even if you haven't worn it
yourself.

Maud Burton's sisters let her have anything of theirs she wants when she goes
to a party. That's why she always looks

so stunning and has so many changes. Mother, tell Bess to let me wear her wrap. I won't hurt your old wrap, Bess. Sisters ought to be sisterly. Don't that look stunning. I think it's more becoming to me than to Bess because blue's my color. What's that? Now, Mother, listen to Tommy calling up that Mr. Saunders is there. That's disgraceful. I'm mortified to death. I'll hurry down. Goodness knows what he'll say. Now listen to him, Mother. He says the whole family are dressing me and I'm wearing Bess' wrap. Mother, spank him, won't you? Well, goodbye. I must rush.

* * *

Oh, Mr. Saunders, good evening. I'm all ready. Tommy, dear, run up stairs, honey. Come on Mr. Saunders. (*Calls up stairs.*) By-by, Mother, dear. What's that, Tommy? My voice is changed? I'm trying to talk sweet? Don't be a foolish child. Come on, Mr. Saunders. Goodbye, Tommy.

MANDY'S MAN AND SAFETY FIRST

("Roll, Jordan, Roll" is the air suggested when this poem is given as a pianologue.)

What's the mattah wid my ole man?
   He and Work ain't never met.
Ef he seen Work come roun' his way,
   Well, he'd be runnin' yet.

Work says to me, "go cook an' sew
   An' wash an' iron an' bake."
My man gits deaf when Work talks loud,
   Scrapes up some kinder ache.

I says to him, "When Work comes roun',
   What makes you up an' dust?"
"He might ketch me," says mah man.
   "I b'lieves in Safety Fust."

MAGGIE McCARTHY GOES ON A DIET

ช ช ช

CHARACTERS:

MAGGIE McCARTHY, *who recites the woes of living with a corpulent mistress.*

MARY O'SULLIVAN, *a chum.*

BIDDY ME DARLINT, *another.*

SCENE—*A kitchen after active working hours.*

MAGGIE *explains:*

Did ye iver work for a fat lady—Biddy Gilhooley? Well, don't. They're supposed to be that good natured an' kindly but don't you niver belave it—they're the tryinest paple in the warld air them fat wimmen. Now, a fat mon is jolly. Well, I won't be sayin' fat—wimmen is all ugly timpered—but it's only whin they're dietin' or exorcisin' or something loike thot, an' thot this last wan I'm workin' for is always doin'. Now, everythin' used to go along pacable enough, until wan Sunday I seen in the papers pictures of fat wimmen rollin' all around on the flure and the radin' was after sayin' how rollin' would raduce the fatness. Well, Mon-

35

day marnin' when I tuk out the Sunday papers from the pairlor the Missus came hurryin' into the kitchin and went turnin' the papers over loike mad. "Do ye want anythin' mum?" says I—"Oh, I was lookin' for a cake recate," say she tryin' to spake careless loike. Thin she found the paper and I seen the pictures. Funny how thim fat wimmen niver wants to tell if they're exorcisin' or diethin'.

Well, I'd forgot about the papers whin I was dustin' the pailor nixt mornin' after breakfast an' I heard a strange bumpin' an' tumblin' and the light fixtures on the calin' was shakin' to bate the band. I run up shtairs an' through the half open dure I sane the Missus rollin' on the flure. Thin she'd git up an' jump first on wan fut and thin' on another, comin' down loike a ton of brick. Thin she'd stoop over an' raise up. An' I was thot scared I says, "Is there anything wrong, mum? Air ye sick, mum?" An' she raised up furious and says, "None of your business, Maggie. Run away from my dure. I was lookin' for me brist pin under the bed," and she slammed the dure shut, but the nixt day she was glad to call on me for she wint rollin' down the upper hall, which is wide

36

an' short and a fine place fer rollin' an'
she lost her balance and rolled part way
down shtairs, wedgin' bechune the side
wall and railin' an' I had to pry her out.
An' she was some bunch to pry, I'm tellin'
you! She was thot sore in all her jints
of mind and body, that she wint to bed
for a wake.

Thin she tuck to diethin' and shure we
was all starvin'—rye bread and lane mate
and no pertaties, nor desserts. The mas-
ter is a good natured mon enough, but
after a day or two he says, says he,
"Phwot's the idea of the scrimpy atin',"
says he. "Has your allowance money
run out?" "No," says she, "but white
bread and pertaties and swates is viry in-
jurious," she says—"and ought not to be
ate." "Look here," says he, "I ain't dietin' (and thrue for him Mary O'Sullivan,
he's as thin as a rail) and my digistion
is all right," he says. "We may be wan
but we've got two digistive organs," he
says, "and mine wants somethin' to ate."
Thin she began to cry and says, "If I
shmill the food I wants some," says she.

"So I must do without," says he, "and
I nade nourishment. Stop that crazy
foolishness. You look all right, "But

37

with the clothes they are wearin' nowadays one has to be a sylph," says she, still blubberin'. "A sylph! fiddlesticks!" says he, "you aint no spring chicken. Just cut out that nonsense or I'll ate at the club until you do." He went out and banged the dure and she wept a few wapes. Thin all to wanst she jumped up—"Oh, I'm so glad I can ate again," says she, "and the nixt night we had a faste—chicken—mashed pertaties and vigitables and soup and pie—and coffee—well, the way she ate was a caution. Now, I see her wanst in a while lookin' at thim skinny wimmen kind of invious loike, but thin she sames to remimber the soreness of the rollin' and empty falein' of her stumick and she jist sames to heave a sigh of satisfaction. She's always grabbin' her ould mon when she sees a fat woman and sayin', "Look, John, am I as fat as her?" He always says, "No." 'Tis longer he'll have to stay in Purgatory fer thim lies. For he's told that same lie hundreds of times. Belave me, girls, if she starts to dietin' agin it's me for a new place, and what I'm tellin' ye is the blissed truth if I iver in the world said thot same.

38

MRS. CLIMBER DOESN'T LIKE NOTORIETY

ठ ठ ठ

Characters:

Mrs. Climber, *who is interviewed by a reporter.*

The Reporter, *merely taking notes.*

Scene—*A sumptuous drawing-room.*

Mrs. Climber *chatters:*

What is it? Oh, you're a reporter from the *Morning Times?* What! You want my daughter Marie's picture? Oh! I couldn't think of it, really. She's *so* young and it's *so* common to have one's picture in the paper, I might almost say, vulgar. She's just had some lovely ones taken. I'll show them to you if you won't ask for them. Now, *promise.* This is one taken in her gown for her debut in a week or so. A French model. Isn't it a dream? Oh, that's rare old lace. I picked it up in Paris two years ago, when I was there. You know Marie was educated in a French convent. This picture in her ermine set.—Isn't it exquisite? All the Parisian artists were crazy about her. They wanted to paint her portrait. Yes, really. That would make a good little item, wouldn't it? What? A fine pic-

39

ture of the furs? Yes, they're very expensive.

No—no—really, I could never think of giving you her picture. Her father would be so vexed. This head would be lovely in the paper—or, well—I like a full length—then you can see the gown to such advantage. Marie is so beautiful. I don't wonder you want to put her photograph in the paper. Some of the girls who do get in! Mercy, who selects them? They are positively homely. What? Take part in this Pageant and Charity Ball, they are going to have? No, Marie is not going to be in it—Well, if she were—she'd outshine everybody—No, I didn't care to have her take part, she's so young.—Who has charge of the groups? I haven't paid any attention, really. Well, if you cared to, you might call Mrs. Richly Rich—tell her you're a reporter from the *Times* and see if there's a place in her group—No—er—I really do not know her personally. You see we have not lived here long in this part of the town (*hastily*). I mean I've been traveling and Marie has been going to school.

There's the 'phone—yes, there on my

desk. I'll just run over my engagement list and see if I could squeeze in a date, and possibly allow the child to take part—What's that? Mrs. Richly Rich says that her group is filled and so is that of Mrs. Muchly Millions? — Well — er — really—I have no date in my book—What, a new group is forming? Well, she might go into that—and if you insist—here's her picture in the debutante gown for the *Morning Times* and then the ermine one, too bad not to put that in—and this head—Well, I do so object to notoriety and to Marie's picture going in the paper, but the papers will be down on me if I give to one and not to the other— so I'll just send to all. Here's the child now. This is Marie—Marie—this is a reporter from the *Morning Times,* Mr. Penman, he wants you to join a group in the Pageant and Charity Ball, and is urging me to give him your picture. What? Why, Marie, you're glad I squeezed you into that pageant at last, I've tried hard enough? How absurd! I do not care anything about it. What, going, Mr. Penman—well, you might take an item or two about Marie. Yes, I suppose, yes. Mr. Penman, although I

do *so* object. Why—er—er we've lived
here three months—What, Marie? We
came from Podunk Junction—Now, why
do you say such a thing? That was our
country house. You go and get ready
for a drive—tell Annette to tell James
to order the limousine—You'll order it
yourself? No, don't do anything of the
kind. I'm glad she's gone. I can't talk.
She's quite incorrigible, says what she
pleases, just like her father. Don't put
in Podunk Junction, please—just say we
have come from our Western Estate;
Mr. Climber has oil interests in Okla-
homa. Marie was educated in Paris—
yes. I mean a French convent. You
might put it Paris—yes—don't put anything about any sudden oil strike—you
heard so? Oh, really, I belong to a very
old family—from—from—why—Oh, by
the way, you might put in about Marie's
gown being a very magnificent creation,
and that we are about to build a summer
home at Golf Links Lake, yes. Now,
really, you've forced all of this out of me,
you reporters are so clever and you do
worry one so. I do so object to notoriety.
Yes—well, I suppose you reporters do
want news. Goodby.

LUCINDY JONES EXPECTS A LEGACY

ŏ   ŏ   ŏ

CHARACTERS:

LUCINDY JONES, *who dotes on funerals and wants to be prepared, when her time comes.*

MARIA MOSELY, *a listening friend.*

SCENE—*A settin' room.*

LUCINDY *just talks:*

Come right in, Maria Mosely, and tell me all about the funeral. Too bad I was took with one of my dyspepsy spells an' couldn't go, fer it looked like it was goin' to be a grand affair. Joshuway Perkins was a grand army man an' a modern woodmans an' them men always turns out good for a buryin'. I took the oppry glasses Murtle Busby give me the last time I was to the city an' I seen the folks goin' from all round in every direction. Nice flowers? My! My! Ten set pieces! Crowns and harps an' wreaths! Dear me suz! I wisht I'd a been there. An' all the ixillary women's society? For pity's sake. Hain't that fine! That good singer

43

from up to the Lonesomehurst choir! Well! Well! I certainly missed some grand doin's.

Speakin' of funerals makes me think of poor Susan Ann, you know, my cousin up to Brown's Center. Wait a minute, Maria, till I git my work basket. Might as well be sewin' while I talk. I want to mend a rip in my old black skirt. It looks pretty rusty, but I'm tryin' to make it do, fer I may have to put on black soon. Course I don't want to look like I was countin' on a death, but you know Susan Ann's been sick fer a long time an' the doctor says she can't get well. Susan Ann says to me one day when I was up there, says she, "Lucindy, ef I die I want you to have my best black dress an' my best velvet dolman with the fringe (course them dolmans is out of style now, but it's good material) an' my best wig," says Susan.

I says, "Oh, Susan, don't talk about dyin'. You're goin' to git well, but ef you should die, Susan, I thank you fer thinkin' of me, an' Susan, be sure to tell the folks here at home about it because in the confusion of death in the house they might fergit it, an' I wouldn't like to speak of it at such a time an' then, too, they might think you hadn't told me."

I was especially glad, Maria, 'bout the wig, as my wig is kinder wore and her's is right good and real nice gray hair, too, an' gray hair costs like sixty these days. So I ain't gittin' nothin' new jest at present, bein' as she is so near death's door an' she might want me to have somethin' else of hern. Poor Susan Ann.

That's one reason I didn't go to Joshuway's funeral, too, Maria. Expectin' so soon to be bereaved myself it might look a little gay in me to be enjoyin' myself. Providence's ways is peculiar, Maria, an' life is a oncertain thing, Maria Mosely, a mighty oncertain thing. Dear me suz! I wisht I could have went to that grand funeral. I'm missin' everything lately count ef my dyspepsy an' expectin' to be so soon bereaved myself. Dear me suz!

GROWN FOLKS IS SO AWFUL QUEER

("Twinkle, Twinkle. Little Star" is the air suggested when this poem is given as a pianologue.)

One time I heard my muvver say,
"I must put up plums today."
I was spinning my new top,
Jumped yight up and let it drop;
"Oh, muvver you must hurry so,"
I said, "There's one thing that I know;
They're pulling out the plumbing store,
It's writed that way on the door.
An' puttin' in a movie show,
All the fellers told me so."
Grown folks is so awful queer.
Muvver laughed and said, "My dear,
Run along and spin your top.
Plums don't grow in a plumbing shop."

AT THE MOVIES

 forall forall forall

CHARACTERS:

THE CHATTERBOX, *an ardent devotee of the screen drama.*

BEETRISS, *with similar tastes.*

MAME, *another follower of the celluloids.*

SCENE—*A jitney theater just around the corner.*

THE CHATTERBOX *tells all about it:*

Hello, there, Beetriss! Goin' to the show? So is me an' Mame. I'm jest crazy about Bushthall, the hero! Ain't he the grand lookin' thing? Shut up there, freshy. That feller says I'd better not walk in the park, for fear of the squirrels. Cute, ain't you? Well, that's old stuff. Come on, Bee, get right in line so's you can set with us. What is that fat woman chewin' the rag about? Because you're breakin' the line? Say, ma'am, don't you get sassy. If we was all as fat as you nobody'd get a chanst. Come, Bee— there's room inside for three more, he says.

Oh, swell luck! Here's two an' one in front. You set there, Mame, an' I'll set back with Beetriss. Don't get sore, Mame. I ain't saw Beetriss for a month. Where are you workin', Bee? To Grabbe an' Soakums? Art Department, sellin' pitchers? Some class! I'm jest in the kitchen ware now. Same old store but a new line. I like the main floor notions better, 'cause 'twas a better place to see the styles. Don't no swells come down in the basement. Look at that dame glare at us because we're talkin'. You'd think 'twas Grand Oppry.

Nothin' goin' on now, but ads. She's one of them tight wads that wants her nickel's worth, ads an' all. Is Joe still your steady, Beetriss? What—fell out? Mame, Bee and Joe has fell out. There's your chanst, Mame. That gets Mame's goat. But she's stuck on Joe, just the same. Say, youse kids next to me, stop wrigglin' an' kickin' against my dress. Oh, here's the feature. No 'tain't. They're showin' some real views. Chili! Oh, rats! Who cares about them Mexico towns? Tell me about Joe, Bee.

What made you can him? Had a row? What, me? Oh, I'm kind of sweet on a "L" guard jest now. Stop kickin' my foot, kids. What did you say, ma'am?

48

They're your kids? Well, you're welcome. Just make 'em quit or I'll call the usher. See? What, Bee? Oh, yes, here's the feature. Bushthall, say, ain't he grand? I love them waves in his hair. Oh, say, I wisht I could act with him, onct. Got four pitchers of him on my dresser. That girl Marguerite Rayne—I don't think much of her. I could act as good as her.

Movie actin' ain't hard. You just go along natchrel like you do every day. One of the fellers the other day said this Marguerite Rayne didn't have nothin' on me for looks, didn't he, Mame? Ain't that a grand house? You get to see how some of them swells lives anyway, in them fine houses. Them are some furs she's wearin'! I wonder if they're hers or jest borried or rented for the act. Ain't he got the athletic shape! The hero loves her an' the old man an' the villain.

Swell, ain't it, to have all them men crazy about you. She sure is stuck on herself. Look at them airs she gives herself. I don't know as you can blame her much with all them men fightin' for her hand. Oh, say! I know that auto will never beat that train. Ain't it great the way

49

they're rushin'? She's tied to the bed post. Now they're lightin' a fire under the bed. Say, I'm just on the edge of my chair. Why don't Bushthall hurry? They've cut away the bridge, an' he can't get by.

Look! Look! Honest to goodness, Bee, it looks like she was really burnin'. She'll choke with all that smoke. There's that old villian eatin' in a restyrant jest as cool, an' him the cause of it all.

I wisht I could smash him in the jaw. Why don't Bushthall hurry? Oh, the train's slowed down an' he's jumped on it. She'll burn up. Oh, thank goodness, he's there. She's rescued. Say, I'm all wore out, girls. Gee, ain't that swell the way he's kissin' her. Where's my gum? I must a swallered it. Oh, no, I fergot I stuck it under the seat. Wasn't that swell the way he got the strangle holt 'round her neck an' looked into her eyes? Say, I wisht it was me.

THE GINGIE BOY

႘ ႘ ႘

CHARACTERS:

THE MOTHER, *who talks of her one ewe lamb.*

ANNA, *her sister, the comforter.*

THE GINGIE BOY, *who learns what a muvver is.*

SCENE—*A home on Christmas eve. Outside, the softly falling snow and merry shoppers hastening homeward, bundle laden. Within, aching hearts that long for the ewe lamb. The Christ Child comes, the Gingie Boy finds a home and Little Dicky's life has not been in vain.*

The snowflakes beat against the window pane with gentle tap— and each flake seemed to fall with icy touch upon her heart.

One by one she packed away the toys, the well-worn shoes, the boyish clothes— moaning now and then like some wounded animal that had crawled away to die.

"Christmas—and no baby—Christmas and no baby! Oh, my God—why hast Thou forsaken me? The little well-worn shoes—my baby, oh, my baby—you will

51

never wear them again—and here's the little lamb—Anna, sister, look at it—that he loved so well—'My ba ba,' he called it and later when he could talk plainer, 'My 'ittie yam.' Oh, I cannot bear it! He was my one lamb—couldn't he have been spared to me? It was cruel—cruel!"

"Sh! sister dear, don't talk so. It is blasphemous. God knows what is best for us."

"And we must sit like dumb brutes—helpless, impotent—"

"Don't dear — don't say rebellious things—you'll be sorry afterwards."

"Sorry — sorry — what does it matter now? Nothing matters any more. Don't tell me he is better off—don't tell me any of those things people say to you when they don't know what else to say. I won't listen. Look, Anna—see—here's the little car—how he loved it! I can see his yellow curls bobbing up and down as he pulled it along—and his bunny! How he used to laugh when we wound it up and it jumped! Can't you hear that merry laugh—and see those dimples? They'll never come into that little cold cheek again—and the voice—oh, my baby, call to me—call to me somewhere from out of the shadows—I'll come—I must come to you! I cannot walk the rest of the way alone. Poor little clothes! I'll pack them away—never to be worn again. Here's the shape of that pink foot in his shoe. How much can a heart bear and not break? And because I was pitiful—charitable—I lost him. Don't tell me—I know. Didn't I bring that little child to play with him from the Home for Foundlings —and now my baby's gone and that wretched little creature—"

"Dear, dear sister, it could not have been helped. It is strange and mysterious, I know—but Dicky was lonely and you asked the little boy to play with him. No one knew the dread disease would come— there was no illness in the home."

"Why didn't God prevent it? Why did He let me bring that child here?"

"We cannot understand—you did it for the best."

"And does that comfort me? I saw that wistful little face every day from my window and Dicky did, too—and he teased so often to have the 'Gingie Boy' play with him—'the Gingie Boy,' that was the name he gave him because of the gingham apron he wore—that I asked

them to let the child come. Oh, Anna,
why was I permitted to bring death to
my one lamb? Don't tell me not to cry—
I must cry—my very soul pours through
my eyes—and I must talk. Do you remember how he loved the little boy and
hugged and kissed him? And oh, sister,
do you remember when he called me
'Muvver' and the little boy asked, 'What's
a Muvver?'—how Dicky laughed and ran
to me?

" 'Muvver — Muvver,' he cried, 'The
Gingie Boy don't know what you is! This
is a Muvver — Gingie Boy — somebody
what holds and loves you a hundred
bushels.' I took the poor waif in my
arms and tried to mother him—and then
God let him bring death to my baby."

"Catherine, dear love, you must not say
such things—you could not know, could
not foretell."

"But doesn't God know — He must
have known."

"Listen, sister dear. I want you to
close the little trunk now and lie down
just a tiny while—just a bit of time. You
are so tired. Let me smooth your
brow—"

"I can't sleep, I tell you—do you want

me to sleep here where it's warm and cosy—and my baby's out there in the cold? You are heartless—why should you care? You never had a child. Oh, forgive me—I don't know what I'm saying— I know how dear he was to you."

"You need not sleep, dear. Just rest a moment. Then we'll talk about dear baby again. There—that's it. Are you comfortable? Close your eyes and rest."

Softly tapped the snowflakes against the window pane. The swollen eyelids drooped and the mother slept. Across the way the bare brick wall of the great Home for Foundlings loomed up bleak and drear. Many childish faces peered out from the windows. There had been a scourge of a dread child's disease some time before and the little convalescents were glad of a peep at the outside world.

One small, white face turned with longing eyes toward the house opposite. There was no answering look and smile— no wave of a dimpled fat hand. The Gingie Boy had been the first to succumb to the disease. How little he knew he had carried death to his tiny benefactor, whose mother, to please him, had asked permission that the Gingie Boy come to

55

play with her one treasured, sheltered baby every day.

The evening shadows lengthened—only the firelight glow brightened the room where the mother slept on. Outside, the snow lay soft and thick like a blanket of fleece. People hurried to and fro bundle-laden, exchanging merry greetings as they passed—greetings of good-will for the Christmas on the morrow.

Suddenly, the sleeping woman sprang half-way from the couch. "Quickly—quickly—open the door, sister dear—he's there—my baby—let him in. Oh—no—I know now—I've been dreaming. Such a strange dream, sister dear! I thought there was a knock and I heard my baby call 'Muvver' in that precious voice of his. Then I rushed to the door and he was there—my lamb—holding out his little arms—then as I looked his face changed and lo! it was the face of the Christ Child. About His head was a halo—but His face was pale and sad. Even as I gazed—mute and stricken—He seemed to fade away and there stood the Gingie Boy in his gingham dress looking up into my face with wistful eyes and a Voice came from out of the shadows:"

"Inasmuch as ye have done it unto one of the least of these—ye have done it unto Me."

She sprang from the couch.

"Sister, dear sister—tell them to send a tree—we'll trim it, you and I—and we'll get out the little gifts. Then you go—ask them to let the Gingie Boy come—we'll have a Christmas for him. It was a message—a message from my baby."

When, an hour later, the little Foundling stood in the warm, cosy room looking at the great tree, brilliant with candles and heavy with gifts—the mother caught the pale waif to her breast. "Oh, Gingie Boy—always—and always—and always in the future—you shall know what a 'Muvver' is."

ODE TO A MANIKIN

("Humoresk" Dvorák is the air suggested when this poem is given as a pianologue.)

Oh, manikin lady, in satins and furs,
  And garments of costliest lace,
You stand like a queen in the show win-
    dow there,
  With a smile of disdain on your face.

Your heart's quite unmoved by the on-
    lookers' stare,
  Who come thus, their homage to pay.
They, wondering, gaze at the glories
    within,
  These creatures of mere common clay.

Do you know, for the wares you display
    with such ease,
  Men have fought—died; have thieved
    and grown old;
That women have sinned for the splendors
    you wear,
  Their souls to the devil have sold?

That eyes have grown blind making cost-
    liest lace;
  Men have drowned, bringing pearls
    from the sea;

That envy and suffering, malice and
    greed,
    Are the outcome of fashion's decree?

What boots it to you, fair lady of wax?
    Naught poor humans from folly can
    sever.
Wars, earthquakes, may come, but the
    styles must go on!
    Vanitas vanitatum, forever!

ISAACSTEIN'S BUSY DAY

☿   ☿   ☿

CHARACTERS:

ISAACSTEIN, *the grocer.*

MRS. WISE,
MRS. GOLDBERG,
MRS. RUBELS,
MRS. MOSES,
} *valued customers.*

SCENE — *A neighborhood grocery emporium.*

ISAACSTEIN, *over the telephone:*

Good morning, Mrs. Vise. This is Isaacstein. Yes, Isaacstein, the grocer. It is so rainy I called you up. Vat do you vont dis mornin'? Ve haf some fine ducks. De rain made me tink of ducks. You ain't a duck. You could not come out in such slop mit your rheumatisms. How iss dose rheumatisms? Only twendy-tree cents. Dat is de ducks—not de rheumatisms. Twendy-tree cents a pound. Too much? Oh, Mrs. Vise! Dot iss cheaper as nobody on de street. Vell, how iss gooses? I don' know vot made me tink of gooses. Not notting about you, Mrs. Vise. Gooses iss first class. Only twendy-five cents a pound. Too high? Vell, de goose hangs high. You know dot joke, Mrs. Vise? Ha, ha! Vot's dot? Oranges? Ve haf some splendid vones. Eh? You are sending some beck again? For vy, Mrs. Vise? Too sweet? You said de odders was too sour. Vait a minute (*puts hand over receiver so* MRS. WISE *will not hear*), Bennie, did you send Mrs. Vise some sour oranges? Vell, she says dey ain' sour enough. No, no! She says dey ain' sour *enough* (*to* MRS. WISE). Yes, Mrs. Vise, ve vill send some odders, yet. Noddings dis morning? Some nice gefiltifisch? Vot's dot? Ten cents' vort, mit liver? All right, goodby, Mrs. Vise (*puts up receiver with a bang*).

Ten cents' vort, mit liver! She must be going to hev companeh. Bennie, send back does same oranges to Mrs. Vise. She von't know. Sour oranges! She must tink I make fruit to order. I take dem as dey come. If she vonts 'em sweet, let 'er put sugar in 'em; if she vonts 'em sour, let her put winegar in 'em. Oh, yoi! yoi! Such a bissness! Mrs. Moses, your little girl iss eating does oxpensive figs. Oh, dat's nodding! She iss velcome, but I t'ought you didn't see and dey might make her some sickness yet. Vouldn't you

like some figs mit your order, Mrs. Moses?
Yes? (*Aside*) Bennie, gif Mrs. Moses
twendy cents vort mit figs, and keep out
five. Her little girl ate dot many. Vat,
Jakey? Some von vonts me on de 'phone?
Oxcuse me, Mrs. Goldberg. I should be
one off dem octopusses mit many hands
(*takes up receiver*). Yes, dis is Isaacstein. Oh, Mrs. Rubels. Yes, Mrs.
Rubels. Your tings dey have gone alretty.
Two hours alretty. I sent dem right
avay. Put dem up myself. Dey vill be
any minute dere. Dey haf gone. I
vouldn't lie to you. Yes, ma'am. I tell
you—sure. Dey haf gone! Don't occuse
me. I am in—no—cent. Vot? In, many
a cent? No, no! I said in—no—cent!
Yes, Mrs. Rubels. Dey mus' be almosd
dere. Yes, sure! Oh, I vill!! I vill!!!
Goodby (*puts up receiver*). Whew!
Dot voman's like a cyclone. She don'
believe noddings vot I tell her. Here,
Jakey, put up Mrs. Rubels' groceries, and
send dem right away! Tell her you took
dem to de wrong house alretty. Bissness
is Bissness!

LIKE PILGRIMS TO THE APPOINTED PLACE

("Rock of Ages" or Handel's "Largo" are the airs
suggested when this poem is given as a pianologue.)

Yea, I have climbed the rugged surface
of this rough old world,
With childhood's tottering step, the merry
dancing feet of youth,
The statelier tread of sober years,
Until I have reached the door upon the
mountain's height,
Upon the very apex of the earth.
And now with hand outstretched I stand
and wait;
One moment drink in draughts of that
pure air;
One moment gaze with eyes undimmed
and head erect;
Upon the panorama of the world.
Beyond the door the way lies downward.
There await the faltering step, the
whitened hair, the skin deep furrowed,
With the mark of Life's decay.
Have I the courage to pass through that
door,
Knowing that beyond I must go down
into the valley of the shadow?

Oh, Father of us all, reach out Thy hand.
I am become a child again.
Savior let me lean against Thy pierced
  side.
Thou who hast suffered on the cross,
For all the countless thousands who have
  climbed by this same way
And through this door have passed.
Then shall I walk by faith and not by
  sight
Until I reach the yawning chasm of the
  grave,
Crying with voice triumphant, "Death,
  where is thy sting,
Thy victory, oh grave?"
Then shall I see with that strange second
  sight
The gates of pearl, the streets of gold.
Shall hear the matchless music of the
  hallelujah chorus.
Voices forever singing the anthem of the
  world.
If I but doubt this lies beyond,
Fear lest the downward passage leads but
  to oblivion's edge,
Then has the climb been vain, aye, piti-
  fully vain.
There is no other reading of the Book of
  Life,

And so with confidence will I pass through
the door.
Not walking carefully with faltering step,
But looking straight forward with the
eyes of faith,
Seeing before me stretched out in space
the cross of Christ,
And still beyond the glory and the wait-
ing hosts,
There at the journey's end.

MRS. BARGAIN COUNTER
MEETS A FRIEND

४ ४ ४

CHARACTERS:

MRS. BARGAIN COUNTER, *so delighted to meet a friend.*

HER FRIEND, *who stops and listens.*

SCENE—*At a shopping jam in the aisle of a city department store.*

MRS. BARGAIN COUNTER *effuses:*

"Why, how do you do, dearie? So glad to see you. Shopping? Isn't there a mob downtown? You looked tired to death. Aren't you well? You look so pale. Positively white, or maybe it's that black dress. Don't wear black, dear. It's so unbecoming. Had such a nice time at your 'At Home.' Do you know I wasn't going, because my new gown didn't come home in time, but finally I thought I'd just go anyhow. And after I reached your house and saw when I went in that it was not really much of a reception—I mean—that it was so informal and nobody was dressed up much, I felt so glad I had come.

"Really, my new gown would have been too dressy. I'm saving it for Miss

69

Flusher's wedding reception. Mrs. Flusher always does things up in such a swell fashion. Still, one really does not have as good a time as at a simple affair like yours.

"Have you bought a present for Miss Flusher yet? Oh, have you? What did you get? A cut glass bowl? Oh, everybody gives cut glass and silver. I think I'll get something novel. Saw a lovely vase on the second floor of the Universal, one of those things that looks more expensive than it is. Then you get the credit of spending more money than you really do.

"What did you say? You've been buying a new rug? For the new house, I suppose. Persian! Oh, dearie, you can't mean Persian! Why, they're so expensive. Oh, of course I didn't mean to infer that —why—well—I thought you might have made a mistake. You know Turkish rugs are pretty and good Persians are so expensive. Of course, I don't mean you couldn't afford one or anything like that.

"By the way, how do you like the suburbs? How in the world did you come to select Glenmary of all places? They say it's the hottest place in summer and the coldest in winter—and then a western suburb, too. Why didn't you go to the north shore? It seems to me I would so much prefer to buy in town.

"Your house is lovely, though. Whose idea was it to have the stairway turn in that odd way? Why, yes, it's rather quaint. Inconvenient, isn't it? And don't you like a larger veranda? Isn't it rather more desirable nearer the lake? But then property is higher there, too, I suppose. Of course that wasn't your idea in purchasing, I know.

"Say, dearie, you do look so pale. Don't you want to go somewhere and sit down while we chat a little. Haven't time? That's the way with you suburbanites. You have to rush so when you're in town, that life must be a burden. You like it? Not for me.

"Say, dearie, I'm going to your tailor. What's his name? Oh, yes, thank you. Some one told me you had a new tailor made and it looked stunning on you, and I thought if a tailor could make you look stunning, I certainly would try him. It isn't this suit you have on? No, I thought not. I thought I recognized it from last year—or two years ago, you had that, didn't you? Yes, I thought so.

"Your reception dress was pretty. One would never have supposed you could make a last year's gown look so well and up to date, covered with net and changed a little. It really looked almost like new.

"How are the children? Some one told me that Harry had given you lots of trouble. Oh, just a little mischief? Oh, I'm glad. One hears such dreadful things—and people always say the fault is in the raising. Elsie—how is she? Hasn't she recovered from that nervous twitching of the face—and does she worry you about her lessons as much as ever? I always pitied you. Children that are lively like yours are such a care. Mine are so quiet. Some one said the other day they were always so well behaved. Of course, I felt pleased, because children's actions do reflect on the parents, you know.

"Well, I must trot along. Oh, by the way, do come in tomorrow. Come to dinner. It's Mr. Bargain Counter's birthday and every one seems to have an engagement. I've asked several and no one can come. We'll just have a home dinner, but I thought I'd rather have you folks than not any one at all.

"You have an engagement? That's too

bad. Awfully sorry. Now, I don't know
what I shall do. You were a sort of a last
resort. Well, goodby—I really must go.
Do go home and rest. You actually look
yellow. Why don't you run in and see a
doctor? Well, goodby, dearie, come to
see me when you can. So glad to have
had this little visit. Come soon, dear—
goodby."

MOTHER MINE

("Love's Old Sweet Song" is the air suggested when this poem is given as a pianologue. Verse only, played through twice.)

The wind o'er the fields of timothy
Makes it billow like waves of the restless
    sea.
As I ride along the road today,
I can feel even now your gentle sway.
The song of bird fills the scented air,
There are nodding flowers everywhere.
They breathe one word—the sweetest
    heard—
        Mother—Mother mine.

And your tired, worn-out city boy
Comes back for a taste of childhood's joy.
At a turn of the road I shall see your face,
Framed by the doorway, that magical
    place.
Where oft you have kissed me and said
    goodby,
Hiding the ache and the tear in your eye—
You smiled the while, that wondrous
    smile—
        Mother—Mother mine.

Heigh-ho! I must have dozed away,
Here at my desk—'Tis no time for play!

There's work to be done. The fever of
    spring
Creeps through my veins, 'tis a magical
    thing.
To the little old farm I was hastening
    away,
And to the dear mother, gone many a day.
In my heart is your shrine, oh, Mother
    of mine,
       Mother—Mother mine.

MAGGIE McCARTHY HAS HER FORTUNE TOLD

ঙ ঙ ঙ

CHARACTERS:

MAGGIE, *who unconciously tells her past life to the seeress.*

MARY AND BIDDY, *her most intimate friends.*

SCENE—*On a Thursday afternoon near the fortune teller's home.*

MAGGIE *speaks:*

Where'll we go today, girls? Sure, it's so late she kapes me, wid all her fussin' an' rag chewin' that it's hard to get out early Thursday, so ye needn't be blamin' me, Mary O'Sullivan, because I ain't on time. If your lady was as gabby as the ould hin I works for, shure ye'd be jist as late as me. I'll bit she hunts all the rist of the wake to kape me drivin' at somethin', Thursday mornin', snoopin' in the ice-chest to see if it's clane an' huntin' around the closets fer dirty dishes tooked away. Bad cess to her!

Shure she found a dish of cabbage I'd put on the shilf an' forgot fer a wake or so, an' her long nose was sniffin' and sniffin'

77

until she found it and thin such a rag chewin'! 'Tis a lot of patience we girls has to have with thim women. Come on, Biddy, me darlint, and we'll hurry along. Now, I've set me mind on goin' some place—ye'll niver guess, where. Well, girls, I've been crazy for a long time to go to a fortune teller's. What's that, Mary? A sin? Go along wid you. Shure it's no sin to find out about a few things ye want to know. There's wan down this strate. Here's the dure. Won't yees go along in wid me? Well, if ye're so snippy fer hivens sake go do your shoppin' and I'll tell ye all about it when ye call back fer me. Goodby.

* * *

Shure, Mum, yis, I want to have me fortune told (*aside*). Oh, the queer eyes of her, I'm half scared like. Yis, Mum, I'll come in. What, go in thot dark room? Well, now, thot's sort of spooky like. No—o—, I ain't afraid. Ye want to look at my hand. Shure, mum. Phot's thot. I'm Irish. Now, how did ye iver know thot? Right from the Imerald Isle I am, and God knows I hated to lave the ould sod an' me Mither and Feyther, who are gittin' along

78

in years. The Blissid Virgin kape thim
both! I hov a good life line? How did
ye know me family was sich long livers?
The Grandfeyther died at one hundred
an' six years. Ye see a cabin an' an ould
woman? That's me Mither—bliss her
swate face, and there's an ould mon sittin'
by the fire? Now, think of thot—and do
ye see me sister Kate? You do? An'
phot's thot? Do ye raly see the pig in me
hond? Lying down on the floor? Shure
me Feyther's awful fond of the pigs.
He kapes wan near him all the toime.
To think ye can see all thot in me
hond! Is there some wan else ye see?
Oh, go along now. A young mon—Do
ye really see Terry? He's a butcher, but
he thinks he'll git a job as a polacemon
an' thin'—Oh, now the saints be praised,
ye see a weddin' and a ring—Phot's thot?
Me fate line? I hov good sized fate, but
I didn't know ye's could see how big they
were in me hond. I'll tell thot to Mary
O'Sullivan an' Biddy.

Ye say I have two girl friends? Think
of thot. Is that in me hond too? I'll tell
the girls ye know about thim an' maybe
they'll come nixt Thursday. Phot did
ye say? I'm workin' fer a person thot

79

don't appraciate me? Well, now ye've said it. It's the truth ye're tellin'. Nobody, not aven the Angel Gabriel himself could plaze thot ould hin. Above me station? Well, I often thinks thot meself. I ought to be playin' in the movies? Shure, I could do as well as some of thim dames. Look out for the girl wid the black eyes? Thot's Lizzie Murphy—She's thot jealous of me an' Terry, but he wouldn't aven squint sideways at her homely mug.

Ye see a letter an' a fortune an' a weddin'? Oh, the grondness of the fortune thot's comin' me way. Shure, the saints must be plazed wid me, praise their blissed names! Thot's all. How much do I owe ye?—fifty cints?—Shure, it's worth ivery cint. Goodby. * * *

Oh, girls—I hod the—the most wonderfullest fortune, an' the strange things she was after tellin' me, Biddy, all aboot me Feyther an' Mither an' the pig an' Terry—An' sure, girls, I'm to hov a fortune an' a weddin' ring.

It's thrue for you, Mary O'Sullivan, I hope to die ef it ain't. There's wan thing I'm sorry for, that the old hin I works for couldn't hear her tellin' me I was above me *station*. Bad cess to her!

IN VAUDEVILLE

ੱ   ੱ   ੱ

CHARACTERS:

BALANCE JACK, *getting over a grouch.*

THE LITTLE GIRL, *with the tabloid.*

THE OTHERS ON THE BILL, *mere fillers, according to Jack.*

SCENE—*Behind the scenes at a ten, twenty and thirty.*

JACK *expostulates:*

This here play actin' ain't what you fellers in the audience thinks it is, all paint an' powder an' swell clothes an' wine suppers. Doin' four a day with a can o' beer and a hand out is more like the real idea, I'm tellin' you, when you commences at ten thirty a. m. with a milk man's audience and then has to scramble out to the nearest beanery for lunch. 'Tain't no cinch climbin' up on a lot of chairs clear up to the flies an' rockin' back an' forth like you're goin' to fall an' sometimes fallin' an' near bustin' your foot, an' that kind of pleases 'em, 'cause the audience wants to be amused. An' then them critics gives you a pain. How they roasted the dame

81

that does the Salome dance this week!
It's blamed hard to wiggle like that four
times a day. They ought to try them
stunts theirself and they'd have some sym-
pathy. Then a real artist like me don't
git no show less he's got a pull. Look
at the "Pork Chop Four" who was on
the bill with me last season. They're
doin' big time this year an' they can't
sing fer sour apples. 'Tain't no cinch
neither, packin' and unpackin', up all
hours of the night for weeks, an' split
weeks, rushing to make trains, goin' to
cheap boardin' houses, or all night hash-
eries or Greek joints, tryin' to be funny
or to make them boneheads in the audience
laugh, an' some of 'em sets there an' looks
about as funny as a crutch. When you
spring your best jokes you'd think they
was in a coffin factory. But, after all, the
spell of the life gets in your veins an'
you'd be restless without it. Then you
meet some folks—there's a little girl that's
been on the bill with me this season.
They calls 'em broilers when they're that
young. She is with a tabloid an' she's
clever enough to be doin' a single. It's
her first season an' everything interests
her. I spotted her the first day at re-

82

hearsal an' she looked like one of them field daisies beside them artificial dames what's in her act. Her hair was red-gold like the sunlight, and her eyes was big and brown. Well, I hurt my foot the first turn I done an' I'd been swearin' under my breath, they can you if you swear out loud, though maybe the folks what ain't on the stage won't believe it, an' I set in the loungin' room kind of groanin' when she come along. Her act had been called. "Are you in pain," she says and said a few little kind things that wasn't so much, 'twas just her tone an' look. The second show between acts we talked while the rest of her act was playin' fan-tan an' the dog man (not a freak—just the man with the dog act) was writin' home. Everything was new to her. She laughed at the signs the stage manager had stuck around.

"Don't send out your laundry till we've seen your act," and "Throw away your horn, let the musicians make the noise." And I explained to her that you might get canned after the first perform-ance. You can't put nothin' over on them stage managers, they're wise guys.

Better keep in with the stage hands, too,
or they'll crab your act some way.

Well, I was just about to explain about
the horn when along comes that upstage
dame who does the single. Upstage? Oh!
that means airy. An' she says, "Never
done but two a day in my life before.
Shouldn't have took this engagement if
I'd know'ed it was four a day," and I
pointed to the sign an' says, "Where do
you get that noise? Put up the horn, tie
your little bull outside," an' she gives me a
look that had oughta made Bernhardt fa-
mous, an' sails on airy like. When one of
the stage hands fooled the dog man with a
call of wire for Bill Jones (they calls him
Senyer Rigoletto on the stage) an' he
rushed upstairs, thinkin' it was a telegram,
only to find a piece of copper wire there,
the girl (her real name is Nell) thought
it was all a lot of fun.

I went to Nell's dressin' room door after
the last night-show an' though it was stuffy, she'd fixed up her make-up table with
colored paper an' her gauzy little dresses
was hangin' over a blanket stretched
against the wall an' somehow the place
looked kinder nice an' homey. "Won't
you go have a bite before you go to your

room?" I says, an' she hesitated. "Why, I am going to supper with Mr. Ekels," she says. That was the manager. I had to think quick, knowin' what kind of a man he was, an' I looked up an' seen Ekels, all dolled up, lookin' paunchy an' red faced an' standin' at the top of the stairs, an' I says, "I can't explain the danger till later. Don't be surprised at anything I say, but there's danger kiddo—see?" An' then she got on her coat an' cute little hat, an' went up the stairs an' I says, "Mr. Ekels, I want you to congratulate us, me an' Nell is engaged to be married an' are going to celebrate tonight." He turned all colors but he was game, an' we all went out of the stage entrance together. He put up a swell little supper at a big hotel an' toasted our happiness.

Nell was game, but when I started home with her she says: "Why did you do that, tell such a story?" an' I says: "Well, Ekels is the most dissipated man in the whole business. No girl is safe with him. If I'd tried to take you away I'd have been canned an' he would have queered me on the whole circuit. Then if you'd gone with me, you'd got fired too. This way he didn't have the heart when we was just engaged to say nothin'!" "But we're not engaged," she says. "Ain't we?" says I. "Why not?" "Why we've only known one another one day," she says a minute after. "Well, we won't see each other maybe for a long time again an' show folks has to act quick. Will you marry me?" I says, an' she looked kind of like she'd say yes. "I don't know," she says. An' when we got in the shadow of a big building, I took her in my arms and kissed her, an' that's why we're glad to be on the same bill. Well, we're goin' to be on the same bill for life after this. The stage ain't such a rummy place after all—I'm tellin' you.

UNCLE JIM AND THE LINIMENT

୪   ୪   ୪

CHARACTERS:

THE STOREKEEPER, *who tells the story of old Uncle Jim's remarkable experience with a bottle of liniment.*

THE SUMMER BOARDER, *the listening subject.*

SCENE—*A country store near a summer hotel.*

THE STOREKEEPER *reminisces:*

Hello! stranger, wal I vum, I'm glad to see ye. Back agin fer the summer? Oh, on a fishin' trip? Yes, fish air bitin' pretty fair fer so late in the season. Business? Purty good—ain't runnin' Wanamaker or Marshall Field out of business yit, but the summer boarders is beginnin' to come out to the Lake an' they kinder congergate in the store an' swap experiences an' trade perks up. Where are ye stayin'? Wal! wal!—to Uncle Jim Holdum's? Ye don't say. Wal, I ain't knockin' Jim but I hope ye git enuff to eat. Oh! Aunt Ceely's a good cook,

87

but Jim is afeerd to give her much vituals to cook. He kin squeeze the gol dern feathers offen the injin head of a penny. Rich? Oh, he's richer'n cream. Ever hear about the joke we played on Jim onct? Set down. Have a chaw of ter-baccer? No? Wal, smoke them little pills if you like. It's a chaw fer me every time.

Wal, I had a young man workin' at the store, who was plum full of the dickens. He's gone to the city now but he was summerin' up here that year. Was a studyin' to be a druggist an' knowed lots about medicine. Wal, he heerd all about Uncle Jim an' how ef—a fly got into the butter—he was so stingy, he'd ketch him an' lick the butter off his feet, to save it, the butter I mean, not the fly.

When Uncle Jim cum into the store one day an' said he was sick, he seen his chanst. "How air ye Jim," says I. "All right," says he, " 'cept I got the dod gasted rheumatiz in my laigs—allus ketches me in the late summer, comin' along of fall. an' near drives me crazy." "Go see Doc Brown," I says. "Gol dern it no," says Uncle Jim, "doctors is robbers. I ain't blowin' no money on bills fer doctors."

88

"Doc Brown has to live same as other folks," says I. "Well, he ain't goin' to live offen me," says Uncle Jim. "I'll fix ye up," speaks up the young man who's name was Charles, though everybody called him Chuck. "I'll fix some fine liniment fer ye. It'll cure ye." No, I ain't spendin' no money fer liniment, young man," says Uncle Jim, "I ain't got no money to throw away." An' with that he launches on a tirade about the extravagant ways of young men.

Wal, I think Chuck was really goin' to fix up somethin' to help him at fust, but he seen a chanst fer a joke an' he says, "I'll fix ye something fer nothin'," says he, "it won't cost ye a cent."

Queer, Uncle Jim didn't smell a mice. He is so all-fired stingy that he overlooked a bet, seein' a chanst to git somethin' fer nothin'. You know they do say that Uncle Jim went down to a vacant house ef his'n in the holler, that's said to be haunted, and watched all night long fer the ghost, so ez he could collect the rent from him. Said no ghost could occerpy a place ef his'n an' not pay fer it.

Wal, Chuck give Jim the liniment he

fixed an' Jim went home. An' this is how
I heerd the story.

When he got home, Miss Lucindy
Jones, an old maid what was a neighbor
ef his'n, was callin' on Aunt Ceely an' her
horse an' buggy was hitched to the fence.
Jim snuck up through the front door, bein'
as Aunt Ceely never uses the parlor but
sets in the kitchen, an' he snuck on upstairs an' removed his nether garments.
which same bein' his pants. Then Jim
commenced to rub his legs. What was in
that liniment Chuck wud never tell but
wa'n't nothin' to injure. But gosh dern
my slats, after a little while it begun to
burn, that liniment did, an' 'stid ef de-
creasin', the smartin' an' pain kept gittin'
wuss an' wuss, till it nigh druv Jim crazy.
Finally, he got so wild he started to run,
an' he run like a white head down the
stairs an' busted through the front door.
He had the presence ef mind to grab up
one of Aunt Ceely's crazy quilts, an' he
started runnin' 'round an' 'round the
house lookin' like a crazy Injun, wrapped
in that quilt.

Aunt Ceely is near sighted an' kinder
deaf an' fust thing she knowed he run
past the kitchen winder, an' she says, "My

land, ain't that Jim?" An' Lucindy looked up an' let out a wild shriek, seein' that the lower part ef Jim's legs was bare.

'Round an' 'round he went an' Lucindy's big shepherd dog, what had followed her to Aunt Ceely's, not knowin' Uncle Jim in the quilt—why, that dog kept racin' after Jim an' snappin' ef his legs, so he had to keep movin' lively. Aunt Ceely put her head out of the door an' says: "Jim Holdum, be you crazy?" An' he shouted, "Crazy—nothing": when I make the next lap, open that there front gate, so ez I kin run down to the creek, an' call off this gol dern dog."

The next day Uncle Jim come lookin' fer Chuck with a gun, but Chuck, he'd went back to the city; an' no one durst say liniment to Uncle Jim from that day to this. Gee, whiz! but I have to laff every time I think of Uncle Jim, an' the liniment, gol dern my slats, ef I don't.

THE FUNNY STORY

ᵟ ᵟ ᵟ

CHARACTERS:

MISS ANGELINA BORESOME, *who has loads of the funniest stories.*

MRS. WEARY, *the hostess who is compelled to listen.*

SCENE—*A dining-room — the luncheon hour fast approaching.*

ANGELINA *recalls such a humorous incident and just must wait to tell it:*

For pity's sake, Mrs. Weary, is it lunch time? Why, I never dreamed of such a thing. I must go. Oh, no—I couldn't stay to lunch. Really, I must go home, imagine my staying so late. Your lunch smells so good, too. I always do enjoy everything here. Oh, dear, no—I must go home—why, I was here for lunch twice last week. Well, I suppose it would be a little late for my own lunch by the time I got home—and I am only going to have stew —I really hate stew, but I wanted to use up the cold meat. I'm afraid I'm imposing. No? Well, I'll stay, as I'm dying to tell you a funny story I heard the other

day—the funniest thing I ever—ever—
but you are such a good story teller—I'm
almost timid about telling you—thanks, I
will have rolls. They are delicious and
that ham—it certainly looks good.

Well, the story? Oh, yes—you'll die
when you hear it. I did, and I said, well
I'll remember to tell that to Patience
Weary. You know I never can tell a
story straight. I forget the point or tell
it too soon or commence in the middle—
but this one—I said it over and over and I
simply screamed. You'll just die laughing when you hear it. What is it? Well
I know you will fairly howl when I tell
you. It is excruciatingly funny. Let's
see, how did it go? Oh yes, it was on a
Monday, no Tuesday—no—I was right
first, it was Monday, because it was about
some shirts on a line. Yes—it—was wash
day and there were some shirts on a line.
Dear me—how did that go? It was Monday. Oh thanks, I will have another cup
of coffee—and some of that coffee cake.
How do you make it? Your maid? Well,
I must get the recipe after lunch. You
won't mind giving it to me? It is so much
better than some I had at Mrs. Morris's
yesterday. You know the Morris's never

could cook. But the story—well, there were some shirts on a line—and mercy me —you'll just die laughing when I tell you. It was the funniest story I ever heard and you know how to tell a story, and you'll appreciate it so much. I am so apt to get right up to the point and then forget it or put it in the wrong place, and this is a scream—I said it over and over so I wouldn't forget it.

Let's see, how did it go? It was Monday and there were some shirts on a line —some shirts on a line—oh thanks, I will have custard pie. My mother always made the loveliest custard pie but I never have had the knack. Eggs are so high now—I am very saving about them. How many eggs did you use in this?

Well, here I am at the end of my lunch, and haven't finished that story. Now, how did that go? It was Monday and—there were some shirts on a line. Dear me— I can't think of the point. All I remember is the shirts on a line, but it certainly was a scream.

IN THE MILLINER SHOP
ʊ ʊ ʊ

CHARACTERS:

THE PROPRIETRESS, *who learns to her sorrow not to always judge by appearances.*

ANNETTE, *her assistant.*

SCENE—*An exclusive little shop on the boulevard.*

THE PROPRIETRESS *speaks in tones denoting experienced salesmanship and her face beams in anticipation of a profitable afternoon.*

Good afternoon. You want to see a creation? Oh—Ah—I beg your pardon. Our's are not mere *hats.* They are *creations—pictures—*poems. You know one's head gear completes an artistic *ensemble.* I have just the thing to suit your petite charms. This lace and fur model—now that's a dream! You look very fetching. Too striking? Oh no. No one but a dainty youthful woman could wear that. Now if it were some big masculine looking creature—they are hard to fit—nothing looks well on them—but you, with those

97

eyes and that hair! Take this mirror and look at the back. Isn't that exquisite? You are not sure you like it? Something else? Oh, certainly. We have so many wonderful confections. Now, here's a Paris model. Just a military touch. How does that feel? Mademoiselle is *charmante—charmante* in that! It is *Miss,* is it not? Married! Not you? Why, you naughty child to marry so young. No —no—don't tell me you are thirty—and have two children! I can't—I positively *won't* believe it.

You want to see something with feathers? Well, feathers are not used quite as much this season—that is ostrich feathers —but then one always likes originality and you have an original air. You never would care for the common thing. Here's a lovely creation. Isn't that a wonderful paradise—so scarce now and the hat is only one hundred dollars. We're almost giving it away. Too expensive? Why, I was afraid you'd think it too cheap. You don't like it? Let me see. Oh, here's an adorable *blue.* You don't care for it? Mm—Mm, about what price would you care to pay? Ten dollars! *Madame,* you are in the wrong shop. *Hasher's Hat*

Emporium is on the next street. Annette, open the door for *Madame*.

Heavens, that poor little wizened faced thing looked like a freak in everything. Here comes a real customer. I *hope*. —Good afternoon—You want to see some models? Yes, indeed.—Just be seated before this mirror. It is a pleasure to show our lovely head-gear — poems — pictures—really, I know you will be delighted. Here is a splendid creation. Just suited to your statuesque beauty. You know it is a pleasure to fit a majestic looking woman. These little thin persons have no style. There! Isn't that a picture? You certainly look stunning. Don't like it? Oh, my dear! Just the hat for you! Look at the back—no? Oh, very well. I have this silver lace model— Nothing like it in town. An absolutely new and very ultra style. This is the only shop that has anything like it—and only eighty dollars—Imagine, my dear, eighty dollars. Something less expensive —y—e—s. I was afraid to show you cheaper headgear for fear of offending you. You have that air, you know, that makes one think of showing you only the exclusive hats. Here's a striking black model. Black is all the rage in the East.

Look at the side view, dear—you carry that off superbly. Too old! Why, my dear—Oh, of course, it—may seem a little somber, but you have a very youthful face and it is very chic. Don't like it? Going to look elsewhere before you buy? We have the largest stock and most exclusive in the city. Of course, other milliners have what you call *hats,* but, my dear—What! You insist on looking further?—Our hats are too expensive? —Well, of course, we only cater to *the* trade. Annette, conduct *Madame* to the door.

* * *

Annette, here comes a frump. I know she hasn't a cent by the way she looks. You wait on her. I am worn out with that big fright, that just left. Statuesque! She looked like a bale of hay. That was too old! Ha! I ought to have shown her Grandmother's caps. What's that, Annette? What made that old frump go away? Heard me call her a frump? Well, I'm sorry, but I knew she wouldn't buy. What! Who was it? Mrs. Richly—the wife of the soap king? And she wanted to

100

buy five or six hats because she is going South for the winter? Oh, Heavens, Annette. quick—My smelling salts—I'm going to faint.

MRS. TRUBBLE'S TROUBLES

☿ ☿ ☿

CHARACTERS:

MRS. TRUBBLE, *an elderly woman who is kind-hearted but generally full of woes. She lives with her son and her motherless grandchild.*

A FRIEND, *who sympathizes.*

SCENE—*A gloomy morning.*

MRS. TRUBBLE *speaks rapidly and with agitation:*

Dear, oh dear, Sarah, I'm all upset this morning, I can hardly tell whether I'm foot or horseback. We've had an awful scene—oh, dear—If Charley only wasn't so hot tempered—dear me. Now, our neighbors will never speak to us again and we used to get along so fine, and goodness knows—I never had the scandal of having the police around before. Oh—me—! What's the matter? Oh, its awful, Sarah, just awful. What's that? You could understand better if I let you in? You *are* on the outside? That's so—I wondered where all that cold air came from and here I've got the door open. Do come in.

I'm just all nerves this morning. Come in and stay for lunch. Won't you? I don't think we have much, but you're welcome to take pot luck. I'll call Tilly (*calls*). Tilly, oh, Tilly, put on an extra plate for Mrs. James. What have we got for lunch, Tilly? Pork chops? Do you like pork chops, Sarah! Well, it don't make any difference—it's all we've got. I'm so upset—Oh, me—oh, my! What's the matter? Matter! Everything!

You see, Charley loves flowers and he had a big bed in the front yard—geraniums mostly and some petunias—well, I think a few begonas and pansies, and the neighbors on the east side of us, the Briggses, have a big dog. Wait a minute, Sarah, until I get my teeth; I can't talk without them. Dolly, lamb, get Grandma's teeth, there under the sofa, pet. You see, Sarah, the poor little thing has no Mother—thank you, lamb—run play now (*puts in teeth*), and I let her do anything she wants and she wanted to play with my teeth this morning—Oh, dear. What's that, pet? Do a cake walk? Not now, lamb. Grandma wants to talk to Mrs. James. Oh, dear, Sarah, I'm so upset. You see the Briggses' dog scratched up

Charley's flower bed and Charley filled
the dog full of buckshot and they had
Charley arrested. Of course, he got out
on bail, but oh—the disgrace! I was just
going to make a change in my will when
the police came. Dolly, baby, hand
Grandma her will, if you're through play-
ing with it? That's a sweet child. You
see Frank had a diamond ring I gave him,
and I wanted to make it even, so I was
going to give Charley a hundred dollars
more in my will, and that's why I had it
out this morning and baby wanted to play
with it. Oh, dear, this has upset me so.
No, Dolly, lamb—Grandma can't dance
a cake walk now. I'm going to stay in
the house all summer and keep the blinds
down, I'm so ashamed. No, Dolly, not
now—Grandma'll cake walk after while
when Mrs. James goes. Why does she ask
me to cake walk—at my age?

Well, you see, Sarah, Charley bought
one of those walking pianos a—pianola,
that's the name, and he plays the Hot
Time on the pianola and I dance a cake
walk. Just to amuse Dolly, she's a poor
motherless baby, you know. Can't you
play? Why, yes, I suppose most anybody
can. You just sit down and walk about

105

ten miles in ten minutes, pushing the thing.
What's that? You'll play so I can dance
and then maybe the child will be quiet?
All right, Sarah.—Now, Dolly, Grand-
ma'll dance just once, only once, lamb.—
Oh, dear, I'm so nervous. Oh, dear—

(MRS. TRUBBLE *dances a few steps of a
cake walk, humming "A Hot Time," dancing in a jerky way and showing by her face
and numerous "oh, dears" that she is agi-
tated and is only trying to amuse her
motherless grandchild.*)

(This monologue was written from a story told me
by a friend and given with her permission.)

GEORGE'S COUSIN WILLIE

ช   ช   ช

CHARACTERS:

GEORGE, *who admits being a bad boy.*

COUSIN WILLIE, *a most proper one.*

SCENE—*George at home, alone.*

GEORGE *muses on the trials of trying to live up to "shining examples." It can't be done.*

I'm a bad boy. Course I know it. How could I help it? Ev'rybody tells me all the time, Pa an' Ma an' Gramma an' Nan an' Aunt Milly. Nan, that's my big sister—well, Nan don't say much 'cause she's away at boardin' school, an' when she comes home first, she makes a lot of fuss over me an' brings me candy an' calls me darlin'. I ain't stuck on that word much, but I let her say it 'cause of the candy, an' let her kiss me onct or twict, sometimes.

Then after she's been home a few days, she's jest like the others, an' tells me I'm naughty and a nuisance. I guess fussin' at me is ketchin', like the measles. I had the measles onct an' they thought I was goin' to die an' gee, you'd a thought I was a king. Ev'rybody waited on me and was gentle as lambs, an' I said, "Ma, ef I'm so wicked why do you want me to live?" an' Ma bust out cryin' an' says, "My precious, you ain't wicked at all, don't say such things." Makes a diffrunce ef you've got the measles, I guess. Maybe they thought the wickudnuss would come out in them little red spots, but it didn't, 'cause I ben wickuder since.

I was worse, I guess, after Aunt Milly come to live with us. Aunt Milly's Ma's sister an' Willie, he's her boy, an' when Willie's Pa died, then Aunt Milly come to live with us, an' she brought Willie. Gee, Willie'd make you sick. I ain't never seen a boy like Willie in my whole life. He was clean an' the mostest properest boy you ever saw. He didn't dress like the other fellers, neither. He wore black velvet suits an' white collars an' red neckties, an' he wore glasses an' he allus looked jest like that from mornin' till night. Sometimes you'd jest wisht he'd fall in the mud an' git dirty, but 'course you couldn't say so.

Aunt Milly wouldn't let me play with him much, that is, she wouldn't let him play with us fellers 'cause he might break his glasses an' 'cause my influence wa'n't good. I don't know what influence is but Aunt Milly wa'n't stuck on mine, I tell you. Well ev'ry time I turned 'round 'twas Willie this an' Willie that, an' "Why don't you get up early? Willie does," an' "You have to rush so an' Willie's all ready for school," an' "Why don't you go to bed, Willie's gone. See what a dear boy he is," an' "Don't make such a noise—get a book and read like your cousin Willie."

I heard Ma say one day, "Oh Milly, it's no trouble to raise a boy like Willie. Now just think what would happen if George was left without a father. I shudder to think of it. He's such a bad boy."

Gee, I wisht I was Willie's father for about ten minutes. I'd feel better when I got through with him.

Even Gramma was on Willie's side. She'd say, "Where are those mittens I knit for you? Lost 'em? Dear, dear me, such a boy! See, Cousin Willie has his." Maybe that's 'cause I skeered Gramma awful onct. I put a garter snake in the bath-tub to see it swim, an' Gramma went in to take a bath an' she come runnin' out an' screamin', an' Aunt Milly an' Ma all commenced shriekin', an' Ma says, "You

109

bad, bad boy. Take that snake right out of the tub." An' when I took hold of it she hollered, "Oh, don't touch it, you dreadful child." An' I says, "How can I take it out ef I don't touch it?"

An' when I got out in the yard I saw Willie sittin' in the hammuk, lookin' like a little angel. I used to kinder like little angels onct when Ma used to read me about 'em, but I'd hate 'em if they looked like Willie. Well, I threw the snake on Willie an' he hollered an' cried an' went in the house an' told on me an' 'course I got a lickin'. Willie's a snitcher, that's what he is, an' I can't lick him 'cause he's my cousin an' ain't got no father. Gee, I'd like to be his Pa!

Say I kinder got even with Willie onct. Us fellers has a army, not Willie, 'cause he might break his glasses an' he ain't 'lowed to play with us, anyway. Well, we was chargin' the enemy an' Willie come along from school lookin' so clean, an' we jest charged into him an' knocked him down an' he cried an' told on me agen. I got a whippin', but Willie had a big bump on his head, so I didn't mind it so much.

Willie ain't with us no more. 'Twa'n't

'cause of that, though. 'Twas sumpin'
wurser than that. Ma an' Aunt Milly an'
Gramma an' Nan (Nan was home for
Chrismus), all went to a swell party, a
'ception they called it. They went away
in a autymobile they hired. An' Ma telled
me an' Aunt Milly telled me an' Gramma
telled me an' Nan telled me to be a good
boy. I think Aunt Milly was kinder 'fraid
to leave Willie 'lone with me, but Ma said
I'd play out in the snow, an' Willie has to
stay in the house most of the time in winter, 'cause he might catch cold. Nobody
worries 'cause I might catch cold. Well,
I played with the fellers awhile an' we
made a snow man an' skated an' snow-
balled an' when I got tired an' hungry I
went in the house. Willie was settin'
readin' a book, "Johnny Jones or, From
Elevator Boy to President." 'Twas 'bout
a boy that was as good as Willie, only he
wasn't 'fraid nor a tell-tale an' he was a
hero.

"I don't like that book," I says to
Willie. "Why don't you read somethin'
interestin'?" an' I pulled "Dead Eye Dick
or The Pirut's Revenge" out of my
pocket. "Oh George," he said, "you'd

111

oughter be ashamed, that's a bad, wicked story."

"Aw, no 'tain't. You'd oughter read it," I says. "Dead Eye Dick could knock the tar outer Johnny Jones," an' I showed him the pitcher of a pirut with a big knife stealin' through the woods. He looked skeered but he peeked inside jest the same. I says, "Gee, I'm hungry! I wisht I had some bread and jam."

An' Willie says, "You know Aunty said not to touch the jam." Willie ain't 'lowed to eat jam 'cause he's got the 'digestion. An' I said, "You don't know how good jam is. I'm going to get some."

An' Willie came after me to the cupboard. "Don't touch the jam, George, it's naughty," says Willie.

"Couldn't touch it if I wanted to," I says, " 'cause it's way up on the top shelf." But the more I looked at it, the more I wanted it.

"Don't you never do nothin' what you oughter not, Willie?" I said.

An' he shooked his head. "Gee, it's too bad you got the 'digestion, Willie, 'cause jam is the bestest thing. Guess I'll get a ladder," I says. "Oh don't do it, it's naughty," says Willie. But I brung a ladder an' climbed up an' when I went to take the jam crock down, it turned sideways an' the jam fell all over Willie, down his waist, an' he started to run outer the pantry an' caught his waist on a nail an' tored it. Say, you'd oughter heard him cry, jest like a calf.

"Aw, g'wan," I says. "Don't be a sissy." But I sniggered when I saw how funny he looked. Then I clum down an' scrubbed off the jam the best I could.

"Might as well eat some bread an' jam now. 'Twon't give you no more 'digestion inside than out."

An' Willie et some. When they all come home, me an' Willie was in the attic, all over jam, layin' on our stummicks readin' "Dead Eye Dick" out loud.

Aunt Milly was mad, you bet. She lit inter me an' said I had ruined her boy, an' that she was goin' to take him away, 'cause I was so bad.

Ma was jest goin' to scold me, when Nan jumped in with both feet. Nan's a brick. Nan said she wisht Aunt Milly would take Willie away, 'cause he was a sissy an' a goody-goody stick of a boy. An' she said 'at Aunt Milly needn't abuse

113

her brother, 'cause if Willie'd play out of doors an' act like a real boy, he might make a man some day. An' I says, "Bully fer Nan."

Aunt Milly, she packed up next day an' she an' Willie went away. Ma cried, but Nan said, "Good riddance."

I was sorry an' I said, "Don't cry Ma, I'm goin' to be a good boy, 'cause it won't be so hard now Willie's gone."

Gee, Willie looked funny with that jam on him.

WHEN LUCINDY GOES TO TOWN

ชั ชั ชั

CHARACTERS:

LUCINDY JONES, *who says style ain't no object.*

MARIA MOSELY, *who can't get a word in edgeways.*

SCENE—*A gossipy afternoon.*

LUCINDY JONES *speaks:*

I've come to one conclusion, Maria Mosely, that the Lord will have his own, 'spite of all our workin's to the contrary. —1-2-3-4—wait a minute—I don't want to drap this stitch—this is a nice patron for a tidy—an' I must say if they be'ant the style, I'll stick to tidies. They give a homey look that ain't teched by nothin' else in housekeepin'. Of course city fokes laughs at them—but land sakes!—we kin laugh at city fokes an' their ways.

When I visited Myrtle Busby she hadn't no parlor at all—just a big livin' room—with ev'ry thing common. Rugs— floor rugs on the wall—a very poor lightin' system—everything dim 'cept

over the table—an' 'spite of all her money
—now Maria, you'll never believe me—
she had a broken marble figger—with no
head, mind ye,—and no arms, that she
seemed to set a store by—on one corner
of the bookcase. I'd a throwed it out an'
I'm poor, but when I said 'twas too bad it
got busted—Myrtle laughed an' said 'twas
meant to be that way. Now the idee,
Maria Mosely, of anybody makin' that
kind of figger on purpose. Myrtle said
'twas called "Victry" but dear me suz!—
it looked more like it orter been named
"Defeat." Then Myrtle didn't have no
soap on her wash-bowl—just some liquid
stuff that run kind of sparin' out of a
glass ball. She said 'twas sanity soap—
but I said it looked more to me like in-
sanity soap—just some run-mad fool idee
of tryin' to be diffrunt from the good old
days. Some fokes would bust if they
couldn't be new fangled. Oh, I forgot to
tell ye, Maria—that there Victry figger
had wings—I laughed ev'ry time I looked
at the thing—the idee of puttin' wings on
a figger that didn't have no head. Then
Myrtle has some of the strangest idees
about picters, Maria. Not a single en-
larged picter, not one of them nice crayons

116

of any of her family—but you'd oughter
seen the things she called water-color picters—you acterly couldn't tell the top
from the bottom. Impressionistic (I
think that's the word) she said they was—
an' I says if you want my opinion—I
spose it ain't wuth much, Myrtle, I don't
get no impression at all from them things
—looks like a jumble to me. Acterly,
Maria, Mis' Mason's boy—Jim, could
draw a better picter with his eyes shet.
She said they was Whistlers'. I don't
know who in tarnation Whistler is, Maria,
but he certainly has Myrtle took in. No
—I believe he was the man that made
some she called edgings—I don't just rec-
ollect—she had such a lot of trash—an' a
lot of fat men an' women she said was after the old masters—looked more to me
like they'd been after a good square meal
of victuals than anything else in the
world.

But that ain't what I begun to tell you
—'twas about my yeller fur muff. You
see, Maria, I laid by quite a nice tidy little
sum for missionary money, an' sech an
idee as usin' it for myself never come into
my head—until I went to visit Myrtle
Busby.

117

Don't make no diffrunce how stiddy your head is—all them pretty things in the shop-windows do have a bewilderin' effect.

Maria—the devil must have tempted me—I seen a yeller fur muff in one of the stores an' do all I could I couldn't get it out of my mind. I never had a real fur muff in my life—an' yeller fur is awful giddy fer me—but that yeller fur was a shinin' in my dreams all night. 'Twas just the color of my cat that died—the devil certain kept busy—ev'ry time I went down town I went an' gazed at that piece of fur—an' Myrtle says to me, says she,—"If you want that muff so bad, Lucindy, I'll charge it to my account an' you kin send me the money when you get home." I was just about to say, "I ain't got no money," when, lo! the missionary money popped into my head—an' I fell —Maria Mosely, I fell—stole from the Lord.

You wouldn't think that muff would have made me happy—but they say stolen fruits is sweet—an' I never kin express to you the joy I had in that piece of fur. When I got alone in my room I'd set it on the dresser an' admire it—like a picter

118

—but my joy was like Jonah's Gourd—
didn't last no more—well, a little longer
than a night—but not much. One day me
an' Myrtle went to a reception an' Myrtle's automobile was out of whack, so we
took the trolley. Myrtle said it was jest
a big Charity Tea anyway an' style didn't
make so much diffrunce. It was a fine
day overhead but sloppy under foot an'
jest as I went to take the trolley my yeller
fur muff drapped right in a puddle of the
messiest mud an' slush you ever see. I
was pretty nigh ready to cry, but I didn't
want to show no extry concern an' so I
shook off all the loose mud an' put the
muff under the seat.

Pretty soon a woman come along an'
went to set next to me an' I says quick,
bein' afeard she'd get her dress muddy,
"Oh Ma'am, there's a muddy muff under
the seat—don't set there."

An' she screamed "Oh heavens —
where?" an' jumped about ten feet,
thinkin' it was some kind of an animule.

I spose sayin' "muddy muff" kind of
quick—do sound strange. Ev'rybody
laughed but me an' the woman an' she
tossed her head an' said, "Some folks ain't
got no sense."

119

When I come to git out of the car I found a newspaper a man had left an' wrapped up the muff, an' when I got to the reception I stuck it under the hall seat, not wanting to carry it upstairs. I 'spose all them swell dressed women—Myrtle said it wa'n't a stylish affair, Maria, but the women was ragged out to beat the band—I 'spose they put everything else out of my mind. Leastways I went home and forgot my muff—an' strange is the ways of Providence—I was took with one of my dyspepsy spells that night an' was sick for a week.

All to onct I jumped up one day an' hollered right out, "Myrtle Busby, my yeller fur muff!"

Myrtle telephoned immediate an' what do you think, Maria Mosely—if that woman hadn't sent that muff in a missionary box to North Dakoty.

You see it was a Charity Tea an' clothes was brung as well as money, an' she thought some one had sent it in fer that purpose. Myrtle didn't tell her no diffrunt—an' she told me not to mind about payin' her—but Maria, I seen the Lord's hand in it all—an' soon as I got home and ernt it from my eggs, I sent her the

120

money. So my yeller muff is doin' the Lord's work after all—an' He claimed His own.

Mis' Simpkins has a yeller tom-cat pretty nigh the color of my muff—an' ev'ry time he walks along the fence I have the creeps along my spine, an' I call him "Missionary Money" just to keep myself from fergettin'.

A QUESTION

("Yankee Doodle," verse only, is the air suggested when this poem is given as a pianologue.)

Where does all the money go?
Who's the fellow gets the dough?
That's the thing I'd like to know,
        Who gets it?

Every month come stacks of bills,
For bread, for clothing and for pills,
Taxes, rent and other ills.
        Who gets it?

The chap that we pay has to pay,
At least that's what you hear him say,
When he brings duns around your way.
        Who gets it?

We know the multimillionaire
Rakes in a lot more than his share,
But still somewhere there's more to
    spare.
        Who gets it?

For great disaster or for 'quake
We must again our pockets shake,
For charity's sweet grasping sake.
        Who gets it?

123

We dance, play cards, for charity,
Send funds to war's new refugee,
Or to convert the bad Chinee.
      Who gets it?

We need not search around for poor,
They're here in plenty at our door,
Yet dollars dribble by the score.
      Who gets them?

Printed in the United States
105189LV00002B/45/A

9 780548 011379